Thank you Jose for all of your support and encouragement!
— Kyle

Dinosaur Archives

Kyle Morris

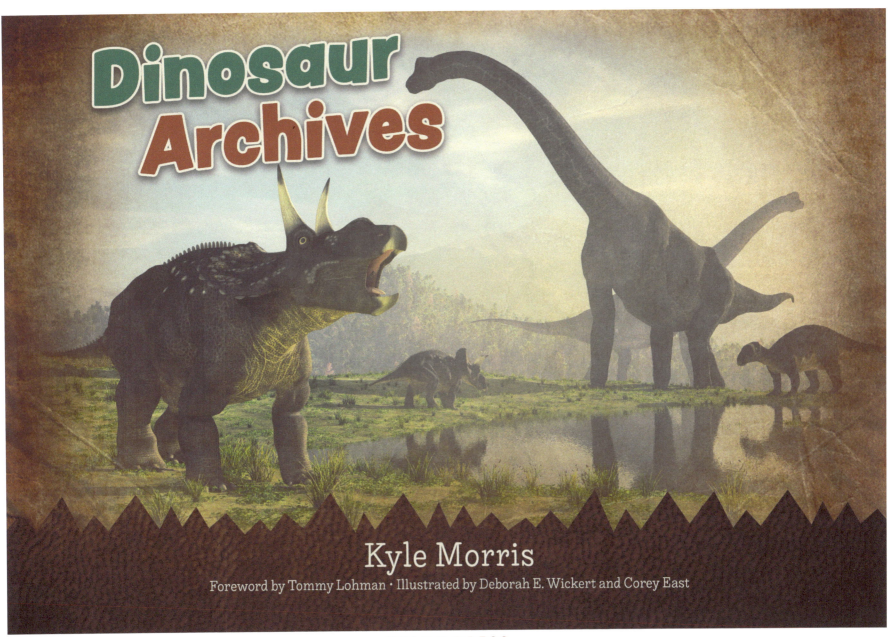

Xulon Press
2301 Lucien Way #415
Maitland, FL 32751
407.339.4217
www.xulonpress.com

© 2022 by Kyle Morris

Contributions by: Tommy Lohman, Deborah E. Wickert, & Corey East

All rights reserved solely by the author. The author guarantees all contents are original and do not infringe upon the legal rights of any other person or work. No part of this book may be reproduced in any form without the permission of the author.

Due to the changing nature of the Internet, if there are any web addresses, links, or URLs included in this manuscript, these may have been altered and may no longer be accessible. The views and opinions shared in this book belong solely to the author and do not necessarily reflect those of the publisher. The publisher therefore disclaims responsibility for the views or opinions expressed within the work.

Unless otherwise indicated, Scripture quotations taken from the English Standard Version (ESV). Copyright © 2001 by Crossway, a publishing ministry of Good News Publishers. Used by permission. All rights reserved.

Paperback ISBN-13: 978-1-66285-978-6
Hard Cover ISBN-13: 978-1-66285-979-3
Ebook ISBN-13: 978-1-66285-980-9

This book is dedicated to "My Little *Stegosaurus*," my wife, Bethany. She is my companion, adventure partner, the love of my life, and my best friend! I would also like to dedicate it to our daughter Isannah. I love you both so, so much!

Tommy and Kyle working on a Triceratops sacrum
at the Glendive Dinosaur & Fossil Museum

Foreword

Kyle and I first met in the summer of 2021 in Glendive, Montana; he came up to spend some time with us doing dig site and fossil prep. Since then, Kyle and I have worked together many more times in fossil excavation and preparation work. During those times, our conversations often turn to the latest discoveries in paleontology, and the importance of defending a biblical worldview to a world that is lost.

During my initial time of meeting Kyle, I noticed a trait that is common amongst those who educate and equip others: a hunger to learn, to know, to grow, and to equip others. As educators, we are not dams, we are canals. We want to take what God has shown us and impact other people with truth and clarity. As you read *Dinosaur Archives*, you will be presented with the truth of dinosaurs in light of a biblical worldview. In the process, you will not only grow by the content of Kyle's words, but you will better understand the passion of the man behind those words.

Dinosaur Archives is a book that I hope will find a prominent place in your library or bookshelf. It will give you a solid cross-section of dinosaur kinds and their unique anatomical attributes, all while being firmly rooted in the context of biblical history. By using a historic biblical foundation, Kyle is rightly anchoring your thinking in the only history that comes from the eyewitness of creation: God.

It is important that we find resources we can trust, and *Dinosaur Archives* is just that. The apostle Paul reminds us in Colossians 2:8 to, **"See to it that no one takes you captive by philosophy and empty deceit, according to human tradition, according to the elemental spirits of the world, and not according to Christ."** Dinosaurs have long been presented to the masses as this grand proof of deep time and common descent evolution; this secular way of thinking has taken people captive by its vain philosophy and empty deceit, according to a secular (no God) perspective. It pleases me that works like this one exist so the deceptions can be pushed back against, by the authority of the Word of God.

Dinosaur Archives is well-researched and honest in its statements about what can and cannot be known about dinosaurs. Kyle paints for you a reasonable picture of what dinosaurs may have looked like, and how they may have acted, without being dramatic or sensational. As a boy, I was fascinated by dinosaurs, much like many little boys and girls today, but resources on dinosaurs written from a biblical worldview were non-existent. This is why I am excited about what Kyle has put together; it is a resource I did not have, but needed. Thank you, Kyle, for taking on this task, and standing in the gap.

—Tommy Lohman
Field Paleontologist and Vice President of the Glendive Dinosaur & Fossil Museum, Montana

What is a Dinosaur?

Dinosaurs (die-no-soars). These creatures have captured the imaginations of children and adults alike. They appear in movies, books, documentaries, as toys, postage stamps, and the list goes on. So, what are these mysterious reptiles? Most often, we are told that dinosaurs were prehistoric animals. The word "prehistory" implies a time before recorded history. However, this is impossible because God's Word gives us a written record of the history of the world, starting from the very beginning. Genesis 1:1 reads, "In the beginning, God created the heavens and the earth." Therefore, biblically speaking, there is no such thing as prehistory, or prehistoric animals. Dinosaurs and other "no longer living" creatures are better referred to as extinct animals.

Getting more specific, some people say a dinosaur is something like a crocodile or an alligator. Others confuse flying reptiles, called **pterosaurs** (t-air-o-soar) with dinosaurs. Still others think they are something like a marine reptile, such as a **plesiosaur** (please-ee-o-soar) or an **ichthyosaur** (ick-th-ee-o-soar). There are even some who think a dinosaur is any extinct animal, including **mammoths**. So, what are they really? Let's find out!

Dinosaurs are a very specific group of reptiles. Just like lizards and snakes, and turtles and tortoises are different groups of reptiles with their own unique characteristics; so are dinosaurs. To put it simply, dinosaurs are terrestrial (living mainly on the land) reptiles, with one of two different hip structures that place their legs directly underneath their bodies. This means that all the animals mentioned above don't make the cut. Crocodilians, such as crocodiles and alligators, have their legs spread or sprawled out to the side and not underneath them. They are belly draggers, who drag their tails behind them, but dinosaurs held their tails up off of the ground.

Pterosaurs, for example *Pteranodon* (ter-ann-uh-don), or *Dsungaripterus* (d-sun-guh-rip-ter-iss), are flying animals, not land animals. The structure of their hips is also different from that of the dinosaurs. Marine reptiles had flippers rather than legs, and as their title implies, they live in the water. Lastly, as already mentioned, dinosaurs are reptiles. Therefore, other extinct animals like **mammoths** (which are mammals) are excluded.

Dinosaur Archives

Dinosaur Beginnings:

Where did dinosaurs come from? Some say that millions of years ago, dinosaurs evolved from other, more ancient reptiles. Then, over time, the first dinosaurs evolved into the hundreds of different types of dinosaurs we know of today. But that's an interpretation, based on people's opinions, not scientific fact. However, we know from reading God's infallible Word, the Bible, specifically in Genesis chapter one, that He created everything in six literal twenty-four-hour days, and rested on the seventh day. On the sixth day, God created land animals and human beings. Genesis 1:24-25 says,

> **24 And God said, 'Let the earth bring forth living creatures according to their kinds—livestock and creeping things and beasts of the earth according to their kinds.' And it was so. 25 And God made the beasts of the earth according to their kinds and the livestock according to their kinds, and everything that creeps on the ground according to its kind. And God saw that it was good.**

That means dinosaurs were created on day six too, along with all other land animals, and the first two people, Adam and Eve.

But what exactly is a kind? The word "kind" is a biblical classification. Put simply, the biblical kind is roughly equivalent to the family level of **taxonomy.** Though, sometimes, a kind is at the order or genus level. The seven most accepted layers of classification for living things are kingdom, phylum, class, order, family, genus, and species. Kingdom is the broadest, and species is the most specific.

Now, when God created dinosaurs, He created them according to their kinds. We as scientists organize these kinds into two distinct groups, called orders, based on the similarities they share. These orders are **saurischia** (soar-ish-ee-uh) and **ornithischia** (or-nih-thish-ee-uh). The saurischians or "lizard-hipped" dinosaurs typically have a hip structure similar to that of lizards, while the ornithischians or "bird-hipped" dinosaurs typically have a hip structure that is most similar to birds. It is important to note that there is no relation between the dinosaur groups mentioned above and the lizards and birds that their hip structures are similar to. We attribute this similar design to their common designer, God!

Being reptiles, dinosaurs are in the class of **reptilia**. The two orders mentioned above come next and are broken down into **suborders**. Saurischia can be broken down into two suborders: **theropoda** (th-air-o-pod-uh) and **sauropodomorpha** (soar-o-pod-o-morf-uh). Ornithischia can be broken down into three suborders: **marginocephalia** (mar-jin-o-sef-al-ee-uh), **ornithopoda** (or-nith-o-pod-uh), and **thyreophora** (thigh-ray-o-for-uh). These groups then break down into **infraorders** before dispersing into different families. It is also important to note that there are both bipedal (walking on two legs) and quadrupedal (walking on four legs) dinosaurs in both saurischia and ornithischia.

Dinosaur Archives

Amargasaurus
(uh-mar-guh-soar-us)

Name Meaning: La Amarga Lizard
Order: Saurischia
Kind: Dicraeosauridae
(die-cray-o-soar-ih-day)
Habitat: Southern South America
Diet: Herbivore
Height: 8-10 feet
Length: 30-35 feet

This dinosaur is what is called a sauropod, belonging to the suborder **sauropodomorpha**, and the infraorder **sauropoda**. This group is characterized by their long necks and long tails. Some sauropods were oriented horizontally, with their heads out in front of them, while others were oriented more vertically, with their heads being held high in the air, like a giraffe.

Amargasaurus, which had an unusually short neck for a sauropod, held its neck out in front of it. This would have allowed the animal to graze on mid-to-low level vegetation.

Like all sauropods, *Amargasaurus* had five toes on its front and rear feet. Though most often, only three or four of the toes were distinguishable from the rest of the foot and had individual claws.

Amargasaurus was extremely unique among sauropods because it had two rows of large **dorsal** spines coming out of its neck and part of its back. These spines curved backward, similarly to how a porcupine's quills are oriented. They were possibly covered in a sheath of keratin, the same material that covers horns in other animals. The exact purpose of these spines is unknown, though it is possible that they helped to support a short sail on either row. This twin sail may have aided in thermoregulation, allowing the animal to more easily warm up or cool down. Another possible use for these spines could have been to help it scare off predators, potentially even using them as a means of defense. The teeth of *Amargasaurus* were long and peg shaped, perfect for cutting plant material.

Another member of its kind, *Bajadasaurus* (buh-ha-duh-soar-us) had dorsal spines that faced forward, as opposed to backwards, as seen in *Amargasaurus*.

Dinosaur Archives

Borealopelta
(bor-e-ol-pelta)

Name Meaning: Northern Shield
Order: Ornithischia
Kind: Nodosauridae
(no-doe-soar-ih-day)
Habitat: Northern North America
Diet: Herbivore
Height: 4-5 feet
Length: 18-20 feet

Borealopelta is a fascinating dinosaur. It is one of the first dinosaurs that has been found with fossilized **pigments** from the skin. This means that we have a very good idea as to what this animal looked like while it was alive. Though the exact color of its underside is unknown, its back was a reddish-brown color. The only known specimen was preserved not only with pigment, but soft tissue, and stomach contents from its last meal were also found, preserved for over 4,000 years. Like many herbivorous dinosaurs, *Borealopelta* swallowed stones to aid in breaking down tough plant material. These 'stomach stones' are known as **gastroliths**.

As a member of the nodosaur kind, it had four short legs, with five-toed front feet, and four-toed hind feet. It was shielded by thick bony armor called osteoderms. These bones, which grew directly in the skin, covered the animal from nose to tail, with only the underside being unprotected. Because of this, many scientists have dubbed *Borealopelta* and the other members of its kind as "living tanks." Nodosaurs lack a bony club on the end of their tails, a feature which is common to the similar but separately classified ankylosaurs, like *Ankylosaurus* (an-k-eye-low-soar-us). However, they made up for this lack of defensive weaponry by being "spikier" overall than the ankylosaurs, with many nodosaurs having sharp osteoderms that commonly reached lengths of one or more feet. These spikes helped to protect *Borealopelta* from pack-hunting predators, such as wolves and raptors, or even large theropods like *Tyrannosaurus rex* (tie-ran-oh-soar-us-rex) or *Allosaurus* (al-low-soar-us).

Ceratosaurus
(sir-rat-uh-soar-us)

Name Meaning: Horned Lizard
Order: Saurischia
Kind: Ceratosauridae
(sir-rat-uh-soar-ih-day)
Habitat: Western North America
Diet: Carnivore
Height: 6-7 feet
Length: 17-23 feet

Ceratosaurus was a small to mid-sized theropod that likely competed with the larger *Allosaurus*, which lived in the same region. However, having a smaller build likely allowed it to outpace the heavier predator, likely running at speeds of over twenty miles per hour. This allowed it to catch prey more easily while not expending too much energy.

They had a short skull, with long, sharp teeth that were shaped like knife blades, which were perfect for slicing through the flesh of other animals. Their arms were relatively long and ended in four fingers rather than three, as seen in most theropods. These fingers ended in sharp claws that likely aided *Ceratosaurus* in holding onto and slashing its prey. Its arms would have helped the animal rise up off of the ground after resting.

Their legs, like all theropods, were relatively long and ended in three-toed feet, with claws on the end of each toe. On the inner side of their feet, and higher up than their toes, *Ceratosaurus* and all other theropods also possessed a dew claw, as seen in many other groups of animals.

Small **osteoderms** called **ossicles** were scattered across its back, possibly helping to protect it from larger predators, or dangerous herbivores.

The *Ceratosaurus'* most recognizable feature is the prominent nasal horn, and its two crests (one above each eye). These features were likely used as a display to other members of its species, possibly being more brightly-colored in males, or older and more mature individuals. They also may have been used as weapons, though they were blunter and more rounded than the sharp horns of other dinosaurs, like *Triceratops* (try-s-air-uh-tops).

Dracorex
(dray-co-rex)

Name Meaning: Dragon King
Order: Ornithischia
Kind: Pachycephalosauridae
(pack-ee-sef-uh-lo-soar-ih-day)
Habitat: Western North America
Diet: Herbivore
Height: 3.5-4 feet
Length: 8-10 feet

Dracorex is a very interesting dinosaur. It was the first flat-headed pachycephalosaur ever discovered. Other members of this family, such as *Pachycephalosaurus* (pack-ee-sef-uh-lo-soar-us), *Stygimoloch* (stih-jee-mall-ick), and *Stegoceras* (stego-sair-iss), have prominent domes of thick bone on top of their heads. Though the skull of *Dracorex* is well known, very little is known for sure about the rest of the animal, with only a few vertebrae having been found aside from the skull. The rest of its body is typically based off its larger cousin, *Pachycephalosaurus*.

Because we lack most of the skeleton, and because they are found in the same area, some paleontologists believe that *Dracorex* is nothing more than a juvenile *Pachycephalosaurus*. This hypothesis is highly-supported, though not conclusive. Therefore, until further evidence is found, *Dracorex* continues to be treated by some as a unique species, and others as a young *Pachycephalosaurus*.

Based off of other pachycephalosaurs, *Dracorex* would have had five-fingered hands and three-toed feet. Their skull was filled with dozens of small, serrated, and leaf-shaped teeth that were well-suited for slicing through plant material.

Dracorex was likely a quick and nimble creature, most often choosing to flee from trouble rather than stay and fight. Though, if needed, the flat, bony, and spiked head could likely be used for self-defense. It is also hypothesized that this animal and its relatives would use their bony heads for a practice called "flank butting," hitting each other on the side, and possibly gently sparring with their heads pinned against each other. This behavior would likely be for play, or to assert dominance in the herd.

Dinosaur Archives

Edmontosaurus
(ed-mont-o-soar-us)

Name Meaning: Lizard from Edmonton
Order: Ornithischia
Kind: Hadrosauridae (had-row-soar-ih-day)
Habitat: Northwestern North America
Diet: Herbivore
Height: 10 feet
Length: 35-40 feet

One of the first dinosaurs ever to have a nearly complete skeleton put on display, *Edmontosaurus* was one of the largest hadrosaurs, potentially second only to *Shantungosaurus* (shan-tongue-go-soar-us). Despite being very large, many *Edmontosaurus* fossils, with tooth marks, indicate it was still preyed upon by the *Tyrannosaurus rex*!

Hadrosaurs, like *Edmontosaurus*, are nicknamed "duck-bills," due to the front of their skulls looking similar to the bill of a duck. This herbivorous dinosaur had roughly 1000 teeth in its mouth at any one time. It had four dental batteries in its mouth, with each battery made up of dozens of individual columns. Each column could have up to five or six teeth, one on top of the other. That way, when one tooth wore out, a new one was right there to take its place. Their teeth were double-sided, having a ridge on the outside for slicing plants, and being flat on the inside for grinding the plants up.

Recent findings show that this animal had a small crest on top of its head, unlike the large, uniquely-shaped crests of many other hadrosaurs, such as *Lambeosaurus* (lamb-bee-o-soar-us) and *Parasaurolophus* (pair-uh-soar-all-uh-fiss). This crest was likely used to attract mates, possibly being brightly-colored.

The front legs of the animal were much thinner, and less robust than their hindlegs. Because of this, they likely could walk both bipedally and quadrupedally. This makes the *Edmontosaurus* a **facultative biped**. Like other hadrosaurs, the front feet of *Edmontosaurus* had four toes, and the rear feet had three.

Multiple *Edmontosaurus* specimens have been found, with skin impressions and soft tissue, giving us a very good idea as to what this animal may have looked like while it was still alive. Some skin impressions indicate *Edmontosaurus* may have had a stripe-like pattern on its tail.

Dinosaur Archives

Fukuiraptor
(few-koo-ee-RAP-ter)

Name Meaning: Thief of Fukui
Order: Saurischia
Kind: Unknown
Habitat: Japan
Diet: Carnivore
Height: 5 feet
Length: 12-14 feet

A relatively unknown theropod from Japan, *Fukuiraptor* was named in the year 2000, and discovered in the country's Kitadani Formation.

Contrary to its name, *Fukuiraptor* is not a dromaeosaur — also known as raptors, such as *Velociraptor* (vuh-loss-ih-rap-ter), *Deinonychus* (die-non-ih-kiss), or *Utahraptor* (you-taw-rap-ter). It was first classified as a raptor due to one of its manus (hand) claws being mistaken for the large, curved, sickle-like inner toe claw, which is characteristic of all raptors. However, it was soon realized that this was a mistake.

Fukuiraptor was a theropod dinosaur, though the exact family to which it belonged is unknown. It does share some similarities with *Allosaurus* from North America, though it is less than half its size. One similarity is the presence of small crests above each eye. Another is its thin, blade-like teeth. Aside from its teeth, *Fukuiraptor* had three sharp and heavily curved claws on each of its three fingers. It possessed standard theropod legs, which ended in three-toed feet, and it had a long tail, which made up half of its total body length. This long tail would have aided in balance, especially while running.

Due to its relatively small size, it was likely a quick and nimble hunter. It is thought that *Fukuiraptor* preyed upon small lizards, snakes, birds, small mammals, and possibly even *Fukuisaurus* (few-koo-ee-soar-us), which was a small iguanodontid that lived in the same region.

Giganotosaurus
(jig-uh-no-toe-soar-us)

Name Meaning: Giant Southern Lizard
Order: Saurischia
Kind: Carcharodontosauridae
(car-cair-o-dont-uh-soar-ih-day)
Habitat: South America
Diet: Carnivore
Height: 13-14 feet
Length: 40-43 feet

This massive theropod roamed what is now South America. It remains one of the largest land carnivores to ever be discovered, along with *Spinosaurus* (spine-o-soar-us), *Carcharodontosaurus* (car-cair-o-dont-uh-soar-us), *Tyrannosaurus rex*, and *Acrocanthosaurus* (ack-row-can-th-oh-soar-us).

Giganotosaurus stood around thirteen feet tall, which is taller than an African Elephant. It had a long body, longer than a school bus. Its skull, measuring up to six feet long, was longer than the average height of a grown man.

The mouth of *Giganotosaurus* was filled with seventy-six long, serrated teeth that were relatively flat, like knife blades. The serrations on its teeth, which are called **denticles**, would have helped it to slice through the flesh of its prey. The teeth of this animal could be over eight inches long. Unlike the *Tyrannosaurus rex*, which had an incredibly strong, bone-crushing bite, *Giganotosaurus* had a much weaker bite. However, it could snap its jaws shut much faster.

Some evidence suggests that this animal hunted in groups in order to bring down and kill large titanosaurs, a type of sauropod. Though its jaws were massive, its two arms were short in comparison to the rest of its body, and each one had three fingers with a curved claw at the end. Its arms were likely used to help the animal get back on its feet after resting, and possibly aided in slashing its prey, or holding it in place.

Though it was very heavy, *Giganotosaurus* has an estimated max running speed of about thirty-one mph. This is due to its large and muscular legs.

Dinosaur Archives

Heterodontosaurus
(hett-er-o-don-toe-soar-us)

Name Meaning: Different-Toothed Lizard
Order: Ornithischia
Kind: Heterodontosauridae (hett-er-o-don-toe-soar-ih-day)
Habitat: Southern Africa
Diet: Omnivore
Height: 1-1.5 feet
Length: 4-5 feet

Discovered during an expedition to South Africa around 1961, *Heterodontosaurus* is a truly unique little dinosaur. It gets its name, meaning "different-toothed lizard," because it has three different types of teeth in its mouth, whereas most dinosaurs only have one. In the front of its upper jaw, there are six small and sharp teeth, with the front of the lower jaw possessing a short beak-like structure, like those seen in turtles. Behind these were a pair of long tusk-like teeth on the lower jaw. And lastly, in the rear portion of its mouth, on both the upper and lower jaws, there are rows of square-grinding teeth, similar to the molars found in mammals. This assortment of teeth likely allowed the animal to eat a variety of food, including ferns and other plants insects, and potentially even small mammals, birds, reptiles, and amphibians. The small tusks may also have been used as a type of display in order to attract a mate, with the larger males likely having bigger, more impressive tusks.

This animal had five fingers on each hand and three toes on each foot. Its tail accounted for more than half of the animal's overall length, aiding in balance. It was likely a quick and nimble animal.

Iguanodon
(eee-gwaa-nuh-don)

Name Meaning: Iguana Tooth
Order: Ornithischia
Kind: Iguanodontidae
(eee-gwaa-nuh-don-tih-day)
Habitat: Europe
Diet: Herbivore
Height: 10 feet
Length: Up to 33 feet

The *Iguanodon* is a fascinating dinosaur. In fact, it was one of the first dinosaurs ever discovered, along with *Megalosaurus* (mega-luh-soar-us) and *Hylaeosaurus* (hi-lay-oh-soar-us). These three dinosaurs were all found and named before the word "dinosaur" even existed!

Iguanodon gets its name because its teeth are very similar to those of iguanas, a group of New World lizards. In fact, initial reconstructions of this animal had it depicted as a giant iguana, with a horn on its nose. This "horn" was later found to be its thumb.

This animal is thought to have been a facultative biped, frequently switching between a bipedal and quadrupedal stance. *Iguanodon* had four toes on each of its hindlimbs, and five on its forelimbs. The fifth digit was actually a giant spike in place of a traditional finger. This spike, which was made out of bone, was possibly used for cutting tough vegetation, or even cracking open large gourds and nuts. It may also have been used as a way for the animal to defend itself from predators.

Iguanodon and other members of its kind differ from the similar and more well-known hadrosaurs in a few ways. Their forelimbs are much more robust, and some iguanodontids have a bony spike in place of one of their digits. Also, unlike most hadrosaurs, such as *Lambeosaurus*, iguanodontids lack the prominent crests upon their heads. Lastly, the hadrosaurs, or "duck bills" have much longer, and generally flatter snouts than the iguanodontids.

Dinosaur Archives

Julieraptor
(jew-lee-rap-ter)

Name Meaning: Julie's Thief
Order: Saurischia
Kind: Dromaeosauridae
(drome-ee-o-soar-ih-day)
Habitat: Northwestern North America
Diet: Carnivore
Height: 1.5 feet
Length: 4-5 feet

It is worth noting that Julieraptor has not yet been officially described and as of yet does not have an official scientific name. Due to this, its name does not appear here in *italics* as it would if it was a genus or species name.

Named after its discoverer Mark Thompson's sister, Julie, this dinosaur was discovered in Montana in the summer of 2002. The "Julie" raptor is what is called a dromaeosaur, or raptor. There are two important things to note regarding this group of dinosaurs. First, it is important to note that the dinosaurs known as raptors, are not to be confused with the group of birds also known as raptors. This includes all birds of prey, such as owls, eagles, hawks, falcons, ospreys, and vultures. The dinosaur group includes animals such as *Troodon* (troe-uh-don), *Velociraptor*, and *Dromaeosaurus* (drome-ee-o-soar-us). Second, due to evolutionary influences and the "supposed" evolution of some theropod dinosaurs into birds, the dromaeosaur group has been "tainted," as it contains not only the dinosaurs known as raptors, but also many other animals, including some birds.

Little is currently known about this animal because only a small amount of fossil evidence has been found, including a nearly complete skeleton discovered in 2002. Raptors such as Julieraptor were predators, and some evidence suggests they hunted in packs, just like wolves. Julieraptor had three sharp and curved claws on each hand and foot. The inner toe of the feet possessed a long sickle-shaped retractable claw that was held off of the ground. This would keep the claw sharp. This claw was likely used to help the raptors pin down or hold onto their prey, as well as cause fatal puncture wounds.

Kentrosaurus
(ken-troe-soar-us)

Name Meaning: Prickle Lizard
Order: Ornithischia
Kind: Stegosauridae
(steg-o-soar-ih-day)
Habitat: Eastern Africa
Diet: Herbivore
Height: 5-6 feet
Length: 15-20 feet

Kentrosaurus is a very well-known member of the stegosaur kind. This group is characterized by small, long, and flattened heads, short front legs, longer hind legs, and rows of plates and spikes along their necks, backs, and tails. *Kentrosaurus* had seven to nine pairs of plates along its neck and back, which became more spike-like the further back they were. Eventually these plates stopped, and the rest of the back and tail was covered in pairs of long and sharp spikes. The spikes were likely for defense; however, the plates probably had multiple uses. They were possibly used for thermoregulation, helping the animal to cool down and/or warm up. Another likely use was for display, in order to attract a mate, or simply to recognize each other.

The last two pairs of spikes, located on its tail, were collectively called "thagomizers," and were most certainly used for defense. Thagomizers from other stegosaurs, such as *Stegosaurus* (steg-oh-soar-us), show evidence of wear and tear from being used. One *Allosaurus* skeleton was even found with puncture marks on its tail that matched the tail spikes of *Stegosaurus*.

Though less than half the size of its larger cousin, *Kentrosaurus* had a unique feature. It had another pair of spikes found on its shoulders. This would have given it extra protection from predators. Not only that, but like other stegosaurs, it most likely had an extremely flexible tail, possibly able to swing its thagomizers in a 180-degree perimeter around its body. This would allow the tail to swing in a wide half circle around the animal's body.

Stegosaurs such as *Kentrosaurus* typically had three toes on their rear feet, and five on their front feet. Though they were likely a low-browsing animal, they could probably rear up onto their hind legs in order to reach higher vegetation.

Dinosaur Archives

Lambeosaurus
(lamb-bee-o-soar-us)

Name Meaning: Lambe's Lizard
Order: Ornithischia
Kind: Hadrosauridae
(had-row-soar-ih-day)
Habitat: Western North America
Diet: Herbivore
Height: 10 feet
Length: 30 feet

Lambeosaurus is named for the Canadian paleontologist, Lawrence Lambe, who is believed to have described the first fossil material of this animal in 1902. It was later named in his honor by fellow paleontologist, William Parks, in 1923.

As a hadrosaur, *Lambeosaurus was a large herbivorous dinosaur.* Like other hadrosaurs, it had three large toes on its rear feet, and four smaller toes on its front feet. The hind legs were larger than the front legs. This likely allowed the animal to walk in both a quadrupedal and bipedal stance.

The tail of *Lambeosaurus* and other members of its kind had what are called ossified tendons. These are tendons that hardened and turned to bone as the animal aged. This would give them a sturdy tail, that aided in balance, and was possibly used as a defensive weapon against predators.

Like most hadrosaurs, *Lambeosaurus* had a uniquely-shaped crest on its head. Its particular shape earned it the nickname of the "hatchet-crested dinosaur." This crest may have acted as a display in order to identify individuals within a group, attract mates, and to differentiate it from other types of hadrosaurs which lived in the same area. In addition, it was likely used for communication. Studies of the skulls of *Lambeosaurus* and other hadrosaurs, such as *Parasaurolophus,* have revealed that the inside of their crests have hollow chambers, which are attached to the nasal passages. This would have allowed the animals to make distinct and complex sounds in order to communicate with members of their herd.

Though the "bill" of Lambeosaurus was not as wide as those of other "duck bills," its teeth were similar, designed for slicing through plants such as ferns, grasses, and leaves.

Monolophosaurus
(mono-loaf-o-soar-us)

Name Meaning: Single-Crested Lizard
Order: Saurischia
Kind: Unknown
Habitat: Eastern Asia
Diet: Carnivore
Height: 5-6 feet
Length: 16 feet

Monolophosaurus differs from other similarly-sized theropods by the single, long, and thick crest running from just in front of the eyes, all the way to the tip of the snout. The exact purpose of the crest is unknown, though it was likely used to attract a mate. Its snout was long and thin, as opposed to the thicker, more boxy skulls of other theropods. Its mouth was full of over forty small blade-like teeth that were serrated on the back.

This carnivorous dinosaur was as tall as the average human, and probably ran relatively fast on its three-toed feet. The arms were short and ended in three-fingered hands, with long, curved claws. These hands likely aided the animal in slashing at and holding onto smaller prey. They possibly even hunted in small packs with other *Monolophosaurus*, which would have allowed them to take down larger prey. Though, there is currently no way to be sure of this, due to only one mostly complete skeleton having been found.

It is worth noting that *Monolophosaurus* resembles both *Guanlong* (gw-on-long) and *Proceratosaurus* (pro-sir-rat-uh-soar-us) and is possibly in the same created kind. All three of these theropods are similar in size, and at least *Guanlong* is known to have a crest similar to the one adorned by *Monolophosaurus*.

Dinosaurs vs Birds:

Have you ever been told that birds are modern day dinosaurs? That the cute little chickadees you see at your bird feeder are distant relatives of the mighty T. rex? According to evolutionists (scientists who believe in evolution), over millions of years, theropod dinosaurs evolved into the birds we see today. This so-called scientific fact has permeated our culture for decades. If you go to most museums, or anywhere where dinosaurs are displayed or depicted, either as fossils, artwork, or lifelike replicas, you're likely to see one or two, if not dozens of partially, or even fully-feathered dinosaurs. But is this really based in fact? Though a thorough exploration into this topic is beyond the scope of this book, we will take a brief look into the many problems with dinosaur to bird evolution. We will look at some of the anatomical differences between dinosaurs and birds, and take a look at what Scripture has to say about this topic.

Dinosaurs and birds are very different animals. Dinosaurs are a group of reptiles, whereas birds are birds. Reptiles and birds are two completely different classes of animals. Reptiles, including dinosaurs, breathe through a pair of lungs using a diaphragm. However, birds breathe through a complicated series of air sacs. This unique respiratory system of birds allows them to not only breathe, but to fly quite powerfully and fast, at incredibly high altitudes, where oxygen is scarce. Some birds have even been seen flying as high as Mount Everest! Birds are also covered in feathers, which are very complex and require a lot of maintenance to keep them clean and healthy. Reptiles on the other hand, have scales, or scutes. Scutes are special, tougher scales that are based in the dermis, rather than in the epidermis.

Finally, a major difference between these two groups is their balance points. The balance point for birds is at the knee; whereas, the balance point for dinosaurs (and most other animals) is at the hip.

Many supposedly "feathered dinosaurs" have been found. But they are all either true birds, or if they are indeed dinosaurs, the supposed "feathers" are shown to be nothing more than fossilized collagen, or other connective tissue found in the skin and muscle of animals.

So, what does the Bible say? God's Word is clear that flying (which would include birds) and swimming creatures were created on Day Five of creation week; whereas land animals (which would include dinosaurs) were created on Day Six. God also tells us that He created everything "according to its kind." This means that animals don't turn into other kinds of animals. We do observe speciation, where animals in the same kind, but with different genetic qualities, reproduce and give rise to new varieties within their kind, but they still stay within their respective kind. Dogs stay dogs, cows stay cows, and penguins stay penguins. Take the cat kind, for example. Over time, we've gotten many different species of these animals, such as bobcats, lions, tigers, and even countless breeds of domestic cats; however, they're still cats, and they always will be.

Dinosaurs and birds: two different and distinct types of animals, and yet both have been created uniquely by God for our enjoyment and for His glory!

Nigersaurus
(n-eye-jer-soar-us)

Name Meaning: Niger Lizard
Order: Saurischia
Kind: Rebbachisauridae
(ree-back-ee-soar-ih-day)
Habitat: Northern Africa
Diet: Herbivore
Height: 5-6 feet
Length: 30 feet

Nigersaurus is a small and unique sauropod. Fully grown, it was only about as tall as a moose, and was one of the shortest sauropods in terms of length. *Nigersaurus* had a short neck compared to other sauropods, and a long, whip-like tail.

Their legs were strong, and their feet had four to five toes. Unlike the feet of elephants, and similar to the feet of other sauropods, *Nigersaurus*' inner three toes on their back feet had large claws, and the innermost toe of their front feet had a similar claw. The claws on their back feet were possibly used for digging nests to lay their eggs in. The exact purpose of the claw on their front feet is unknown.

The most unusual aspect of this dinosaur is its skull. Unlike other sauropods that had a boxy skull, such as *Camarasaurus* (cuh-mare-uh-soar-us), or a long and thin skull like *Diplodocus* (dih-plod-uh-kiss), the skull of *Nigersaurus* was shaped like a vacuum cleaner. This design caused the animal's mouth to be much wider than the rest of its head. This wide mouth had more than 500 teeth arranged into two dental batteries. Each jaw, both upper and lower, had one battery at the front of the jaw. The upper battery was made up of about sixty columns of teeth. Each column, in turn, had multiple replacement teeth stacked on top of one another. The lower battery had about sixty-eight columns, and each column also contained numerous replacement teeth. The exposed and usable teeth were replaced often, and this wide mouth full of hundreds of teeth allowed the animal to easily eat large bites of grass, ferns, and other low-lying plants.

Dinosaur Archives

Oviraptor
(oh-vih-rap-ter)

Name Meaning: Egg Thief
Order: Saurischia
Kind: Oviraptoridae
(oh-vih-rap-ter-ih-day)
Habitat: Eastern Asia
Diet: Omnivore
Height: 3 feet
Length: 5-6 feet

No other dinosaur has a more deceptive name than the *Oviraptor*. This unique-looking theropod was originally given its name, meaning "egg thief," due to the first remains discovered being found near a nest of fossilized eggs. Early paleontologists thought that the animal was possibly stealing the eggs for food. However, further analysis of another nest with an *Oviraptor* crouched on top, which included the discovery of an *Oviraptor* embryo inside one of the eggs, indicated that the eggs belonged to the *Oviraptor* itself. The mother was likely buried in flood water and sediment in the Global Flood, while in the act of laying her eggs.

The second half of its name is also misleading. Though "raptor" is in its name, it is not at all related to the dromaeosaurs such as *Velociraptor*. As such, it lacks the "killer claw" that the true raptors are known for.

Oviraptor had a large crest on top of its head, which was likely used as a display for attracting a mate. It was equipped with a toothless, turtle-like beak, which would have allowed it to easily clip leaves and other plant matter from branches. In addition, this beak may have been used to crush nuts and hard fruits like melons. Though thought to be primarily an herbivore, *Oviraptors* apparently supplemented their diets with small animals, evidenced by one individual found with a small lizard in its stomach.

This small dinosaur had long arms in proportion to its overall body size. These arms ended in three-fingered hands, with small claws. Like all theropods, each foot had three toes to support its weight and aid in balance. While not a very large dinosaur, its long legs suggest it could run quite swiftly. Some estimates place its max speed at forty mph.

Plateosaurus
(plat-ee-oh-soar-us)

Name Meaning: Broad Lizard
Order: Saurischia
Kind: Plateosauridae
(plat-ee-oh-soar-ih-day)
Habitat: Europe
Diet: Herbivore
Height: 7-8 feet
Length: 30-32 feet

Plateosaurus is a member of the suborder sauropodomorpha. This group is further broken down into the infraorders of sauropoda and prosauropoda. *Plateosaurus* belongs to a group known as prosauropods. These animals share similarities with the sauropods, but unlike sauropods, prosauropods had small forelimbs compared to their hindlimbs, and were likely bipedal.

It's important to pause and understand that some secular scientists believe that the prosauropods evolved into the much larger and more diverse sauropods. However, Scripture is clear that animals can only produce offspring with fellow members of their kind. Therefore, one kind cannot "evolve" into another kind.

The *Plateosaurus*'s tail was as long as the rest of its body. Its neck was long and flexible, and its head was small in comparison to the rest of its body. The skull was somewhat rectangular in shape, and much longer than it was tall. Its jaws held about 100 serrated, leaf-shaped teeth for cutting plant material. Due to the position of the lower jaw, it is thought that *Plateosaurus* had a strong jaw. This, along with the shape of its teeth, helped it to cut, crush, and slice through tough plant material, such as tree leaves and ferns.

Their arms reached lengths of three to four feet long and ended in five-fingered hands. The fourth and fifth digits were considerably smaller than the other three. These three larger fingers ended in large, curved claws. The hands of *Plateosaurus* were likely used to grasp branches and pull them close enough for the animal to feed, and their claws may have been used to slash at attacking predators.

The legs of this animal were longer than its arms and ended in five-toed feet. As in the *Plateosaurus'* hands, the outer two toes were smaller than the other three. Their legs would have been strong and muscular, ideal for making quick getaways from large predators, or groups of smaller predators.

Qianzhousaurus
(key-on-sue-soar-us)

Name Meaning: Qianzhou Lizard
Order: Saurischia
Kind: Tyrannosauridae
(tie-ran-oh-soar-ih-day)
Habitat: Eastern Asia
Diet: Carnivore
Height: 7-8 feet
Length: 20-23 feet

Qianzhousaurus is an oddity when it comes to tyrannosaurs. Unlike larger members of its kind, such as the Asian *Tarbosaurus* (tar-bow-soar-us) and the North American *Tyrannosaurus rex*, which have broad, yet relatively short snouts, *Qianzhousaurus* had an incredibly long snout. Its snout is so long that it's been nicknamed the "Pinnochio rex." In fact, the snout takes up about seventy percent of the entire skull.

The skull of this predator wasn't very wide or deep. This meant that there was not much room for muscle attachment. Therefore, unlike other tyrannosaurs, which are known for their incredibly strong bites, *Qianzhousaurus* had a relatively weak bite by comparison. Its teeth were thin and serrated, like steak knives, which is different from the typical "railroad spike" teeth of its larger cousins. This makes sense, because without a bone-crushing bite, there's no need for bone-piercing teeth. Rather, the teeth of *Qianzhousaurus* were better suited for slicing the flesh of its prey.

The rest of this dinosaur was slimly-built as well. Its legs were long and slender, likely allowing the animal to chase down quick and nimble prey.

At the time of publishing, the forelimbs of *Qianzhousaurus* are yet unknown. Though, since it is classified as a tyrannosaur, it can be assumed that they had short arms, that ended in two-fingered hands.

Though larger, *Qianzhousaurus* is very similar to another tyrannosaur found in Asia, *Alioramus*. It is possible that *Alioramus* was a young adult or juvenile *Qianzhousaurus*.

Dinosaur Archives

Rajasaurus
(rah-ja-soar-us)

Name Meaning: Princely Lizard
Order: Saurischia
Kind: Abelisauridae
(uh-bell-ih-soar-ih-day)
Habitat: India
Diet: Carnivore
Height: 6.5-8 feet
Length: 20-25 feet

Sometimes called the "bull dogs" of the dinosaur world, abelisaurs are a very unique group of theropod dinosaurs. *Rajasaurus* was a small to mid-sized member of this group that lived in what is now India.

It had a short, but heavily-built skull, that was only two feet in length. A similar, small but strong, skull is found in other abelisaurs, such as the African *Majungasaurus* (muh-jun-guh-soar-us) and the well-known South American *Carnotaurus* (car-no-tore-us). The skull of *Rajasaurus* was filled with numerous small, thin, and blade-like teeth. These teeth were well-adapted for slicing into the flesh of its prey, though they could not cut very deep, due to their small size.

Another unique feature of this animal is the presence of a single, small crest on the top of its head, located between the eyes. Unlike other crested theropods, the crest of *Rajasaurus* is strangely small, being only a single inch in height. This crest was likely used as a display, potentially to attract a mate. Males may have had larger and more brightly-colored crests in order to attract females. We see similar "showy" ornamentations in many of the reptiles that are still around today.

Though the forelimbs of *Rajasaurus* have not yet been found, it likely had incredibly short arms, like those found on *Majungasaurus* and *Carnotaurus*. A unique trait of the arms of these animals is that they had four fingers, rather than the typical three found in most theropods.

Their tail was thick and slightly longer than the rest of its body. This design is perfect for counterbalance, allowing the animal to remain balanced while walking, running, and of course, standing still. Their long and stocky legs likely allowed them to sprint at high speeds, chasing down smaller prey.

Suchomimus
(sue-co-my-miss)

Name Meaning: Crocodile Mimic
Order: Saurischia
Kind: Spinosauridae
(spine-oh-soar-ih-day)
Habitat: Northern Africa
Diet: Carnivore
Height: 9-10 feet
Length: 32-36 feet

Suchomimus belongs to a group of theropod dinosaurs known as spinosaurids. Other members of this group include *Irritator* (ear-ih-tate-er), *Baryonyx* (berry-on-ix), and of course, *Spinosaurus*, after which the kind gets its name.

As its name suggests, *Suchomimus* shares many similarities with crocodilians, like crocodiles and gharials. *Suchomimus* and the other members of its kind exhibit long, slender snouts, and conical teeth, similar to crocodilians. They also exhibit large robust forelimbs with three-fingered hands. These hands ended in long, curved claws. All three of these features combined make the spinosaurids perfectly adapted for life as **piscivores** (pie-si-vor). Piscivores are a specialized type of carnivore that primarily hunt and eat fish.

The back of *Suchomimus* had a low, sail-like ridge, due to some of its dorsal (back), sacral (hip), and caudal (tail) vertebrae being unusually tall. The structure was tallest above the hip of the animal. The exact purpose of this "sail" is unknown.

This dinosaur is the second largest of the spinosaurs, ranking just behind the larger *Spinosaurus*. Though some scientists would argue that the *Oxalaia* (ox-uh-lie-uh) from Brazil is its own genus, which would make it the second largest spinosaur. However, "*Oxalaia*" is known from extremely fragmentary fossil material, and is most likely nothing more than a juvenile *Spinosaurus*.

Suchomimus' long and slender jaw was filled with approximately 120 conical teeth that curved backwards. This design would have helped to prevent fish and other prey from backing out of the predator's mouth. The more the prey struggled to get free, the further it would imbed itself into the teeth of the predator.

The front of the upper jaw had an interesting kink in it. The lower jaw had an upwardly curved tip that would fit into this kink. The nostrils, referred to as nares, were further back on the skull than in other non-spinosaurid theropods. On the top of the skull and above the eyes, there was a single bony ridge, or crest.

Dinosaur Archives

Therizinosaurus
(ther-ih-zeen-oh-soar-us)

Name Meaning: Scythe Lizard
Order: Saurischia
Kind: Therizinosauridae
(ther-ih-zeen-oh-soar-ih-day)
Habitat: Eastern Asia
Diet: Herbivore
Height: 18 feet
Length: 30 feet

Therizinosaurus is a very distinctive dinosaur. Though undoubtedly a theropod, *Therizinosaurus* and the other members of its kind belong to the infraorder called therizinosauria. This group is unique in that they were herbivores, and they stood more upright than other theropods, using their long necks for reaching plant material high up in trees or bushes.

Though each species within this kind had three moderately long claws on the end of their three-fingered hands, *Therizinosaurus* had the longest by far. This is actually where it gets its name, which means "scythe lizard," due to its enormous claws resembling a sickle or scythe used for harvesting crops. In fact, *Therizinosaurus* had the longest known claws of any animal to ever live, with the largest reaching over thirty-six inches, or three feet in length. These claws were stiff and covered in a sheath of keratin. The exact purpose of these claws is unknown, though several theories exist. It is possible that they were used as a sign of maturity, with older individuals having larger claws. They may also have been used to reach and manipulate plant matter, such as fruits high up in trees. Lastly, they were likely used as a form of defense and intimidation, as most predators would not want to attack something with claws this big.

Though the skull is currently unknown, its overall shape can be inferred (guessed) based on its smaller cousins, mainly *Erlikosaurus* (er-lick-oh-soar-us). Based on this smaller member of its kind, *Therizinosaurus* likely had a hard beak-like structure at the front of its mouth for clipping and cutting off leaves, and other plant material. Its teeth would have been small and peg like.

Its legs were long, reaching lengths of over nine feet, and their feet had three toes; however, the dew claw was much closer to the ground than is usually seen in theropods. Its arms, which held those massive hands, were over seven feet long, and incredibly muscular. Based on its smaller relatives, its tail would be close to half the length of its entire body, at about thirteen feet long.

Utahraptor
(you-taw-rap-ter)

Name Meaning: Utah's Predator
Order: Saurischia
Kind: Dromaeosauridae
(drome-ee-o-soar-ih-day)
Habitat: Western North America
Diet: Carnivore
Height: 5-6 feet
Length: 15-20 feet

First discovered in the U.S. state of Utah, this dinosaur will go down in history as the real raptor from *Jurassic Park*. While called *Velociraptors* in the films, the real-world *Velociraptor* was actually from Mongolia, and was less than half the size of the raptors in the films. However, the size of the movie raptors matches up very nicely with the size of the *Utahraptor*.

This animal was a large dromaeosaur, or raptor. In fact, *Utahraptor* is the largest known member of the raptor kind. Standing as tall as the average adult man, they likely weighed close to half a ton, or 1,000 pounds. That's about as heavy as some grizzly bears.

Unlike the smaller members of its kind, such as *Deinonychus*, *Velociraptor*, and *Julieraptor*, the *Utahraptor* was built more for strength than for speed. Their leg bones were much thicker by comparison, and this likely allowed them to deliver powerful kicks to their prey. The "killer-claw" on their inner toe could reach up to nine inches long. This claw was retractable, as were the inner toe claws of all dromaeosaurs. This unique trait was likely used for pinning smaller prey down, latching onto the backs of larger animals, and for delivering fatal blows. The inner toe would have been held in a retracted position when not in use to keep the claw from becoming dull by scraping along the ground.

Though it wasn't necessarily designed for speed, *Utahraptor* was certainly still quick enough to chase down most prey. Its long arms, with their sharp claws, would have allowed it to grasp onto its prey and hold on, possibly pulling it to the ground. Its skull was filled with dozens of thin, serrated, blade-like teeth that were perfect for cutting and slicing. Their long tail would have aided the animal in balancing, and allowed it to be more agile. Though they didn't necessarily need to, it's possible that *Utahraptor* traveled and hunted in packs or family groups in order to take down larger prey, and defend against larger predators, including predatory dinosaurs like *Ceratosaurus* and *Allosaurus*.

Dinosaur Archives

Velociraptor
(vuh-loss-ih-rap-ter)

Name Meaning: Swift Thief
Order: Saurischia
Kind: Dromaeosauridae
Habitat: Eastern Asia
Diet: Carnivore
Height: 1.5-2 feet
Length: 6-7 feet

Velociraptor is a name that strikes fear into the hearts of many children and adults alike. This is due to its "starring role" in the *Jurassic Park* franchise. However, the creature portrayed in the films more closely resembles the *Velociraptor's* larger cousin, the *Utahraptor*, both in size and body shape.

At about one and a half to two feet in height, *Velociraptor* was around the size of a large male turkey. This small size may have caused them to hunt in packs, allowing them to take down larger prey.

This small theropod dinosaur was unique among dromaeosaurs, in that its skull was low, and long, with its snout curved upward rather than downward. Its jaws were filled with around fifty small, serrated, and backwards-curving teeth. This design is perfect for slicing, and the backward orientation of the teeth would help to prevent struggling prey from escaping.

The arms and legs of *Velociraptor* were similar to those of other raptors. Their arms were long, with long fingers that ended in sharp, curved claws. Their legs were long and slender, likely allowing the animal to run at great speeds. Their stiff tail, a rare attribute in theropods, would have aided in balancing the animal as it ran, letting it make swift and agile turns.

Finally, as with all other raptors, their long legs ended in three-toed feet. Each toe was equipped with a large claw that would help the animal grip the ground. The inner toe, however, was armed with a much larger "killer claw." The inner-toe claw was over three inches long and was curved like a sickle. Retractable and held off of the ground when not in use, the inner toe claw was likely used to pin down small prey animals, or to puncture deep into the bodies of larger animals. This claw was better suited for stabbing, rather than slashing, as it was not sharp on the inner edge.

Did you know, the *Velociraptor* and *Deinonychus* have a hip structure that is unique compared to most theropods? Their pubis bone (one of three bones that make up their hips) faces backward, toward the tail of the animal, rather than forward, as seen in most other raptors, and most theropods in general.

Wendiceratops
(wendy-s-air-uh-tops)

Name Meaning: Wendy's Horn Face
Order: Ornithischia
Kind: Ceratopsidae
Habitat: Northern North America
Diet: Herbivore
Height: 7-8 feet
Length: 20 feet

Wendiceratops belongs to a group of dinosaurs known as ceratopsians. Well-known examples include *Triceratops*, *Styracosaurus* (sty-rack-oh-soar-us), and *Pentaceratops* (pen-tuh-s-air-uh-tops). This famous group of animals are characterized by walking on all fours, having massive heads, and bony, shield-like frills. They are also known for their large and often ornamental horns found on their skulls. Ceratopsians showcase some of the largest amounts of diversity among any of the dinosaur kinds, with various body sizes, amounts of horns, horn shapes, and even frill shapes. Many ceratopsians (including *Wendiceratops*) have been found in bonebeds with multiple individuals, leading some paleontologists to believe that they lived in herds.

Named after its discoverer, Wendy Sloboda, *Wendiceratops* is a very unique ceratopsian. Unlike many of the other members of its kind, which had long, pointed nasal horns, the nasal or "nose" horn of *Wendiceratops* appears to have been low and blunt. Its skull was up to several feet in length, and its large bony frill was curved in shape. Lining the edge of its frill were several bony protrusions, called **epoccipitals**. In *Wendiceratops*, several of these protrusions curved inward and down. The exact purpose of this ornamentation is unknown, though one possibility is that, just like the antlers of a deer, these spikes could have been used for identifying different species, or even for recognizing individuals within a species.

Though fossil evidence of the eyes, called orbits, and the surrounding skull has not yet been found, most paleontologists believe that *Wendiceratops* possessed two forward-facing brow horns, as seen in many other ceratopsians. However, this is unconfirmed, and if true, the exact shape of these horns is unknown.

The legs of *Wendiceratops* were relatively short and robust. They were undoubtedly designed for bearing large amounts of weight. These legs ended in five toes that were likely encased in a "mitten" of flesh, similarly to the legs of elephants and rhinoceroses. This means that the individual toes were likely barely distinguishable from one another.

The tail of *Wendiceratops* was short like the tails of other ceratopsians, accounting for about one third of the animal's total length.

Xenoceratops
(z-know-s-air-uh-tops)

Name Meaning: Alien Horned Face
Order: Ornithischia
Kind: Ceratopsidae
Habitat: Northern North America
Diet: Herbivore
Height: 7-8 feet
Length: 20 feet

Xenoceratops gets its name because it was found in the Foremost Formation, a geological formation in a region of Alberta, Canada where no ceratopsians had yet been found.

Though only known from an incomplete skull, like all other ceratopsians, *Xenoceratops* had a large head with a bony frill. The spikes adorning this animal's frill were unique. At the highest point, and on either side of the frill there were large horn-like spikes. Next to these, on the inner side of the frill, were large, bony knobs. These unique frill ornamentations point to the incredible amount of diversity within the ceratopsian kind, and indeed show the creativity of their Creator.

The front portion of the skull is not fully known, though it appeared to have large brow horns above the eyes and a low nasal horn. This low horn was likely very blunt, and may have been similar to the "nasal boss" seen in another ceratopsian called *Pachyrhinosaurus* (pack-ee-rhino-soar-us). Unlike most ceratopsians, *Pachyrhinosaurus* did not possess any facial horns, but rather had a large mass of bone (called a nasal boss) above its nostrils, and to the front of the eyes.

Because the rest of the skeleton has not yet been found, the exact size of *Xenoceratops* is unknown, but based on the dimensions of the skull, it appears to have been similar in size to the *Wendiceratops*.

Yutyrannus
(you-tie-ran-iss)

Name Meaning: Feathered Tyrant
Order: Saurischia
Kind: Unknown
Habitat: Eastern Asia
Diet: Carnivore
Height: 9 feet
Length: 30 feet

Yutyrannus is mostly known for the supposed "feathers" found on parts of the animal's body. These "feathers" are heralded by secular paleontologists as direct evidence that theropod dinosaurs gave rise to modern birds. A closer look at these so-called "feathers," however, tells us that they are nearly identical in structure to **collagen fibers** that have been exposed to water for an extended period of time. This makes sense in the context of the catastrophic, global flood described in Genesis.

This dinosaur was far from the fluffy theropod it is often depicted as. Like all dinosaurs, *Yutyrannus* would have been covered in thick, scaly skin, as evidenced by fossilized skin impressions found with many other dinosaurs, such as *Edmontosaurus* and *Carnotaurus*.

Around the same size as the more well-known *Allosaurus*, *Yutyrannus* had long arms that ended in three-fingered hands, with large, curved claws. These arms were likely very robust, and aided the animal in rising from a resting position, as well as holding prey in place. Its tail, though comparable in length, was significantly thinner than the tail of an equally-sized *Allosaurus*.

The legs of *Yutyrannus* were similar in length and shape to those of other similarly-sized theropods. They ended in three clawed toes. These powerful legs would have allowed the animal to chase down smaller prey. With all three *Yutyrannus* fossils found to date having been found together, it's possible that *Yutyrannus* sometimes hunted in packs, or small family groups.

Finally, the skull of *Yutyrannus* was unique. Though similar in the overall shape to the skull of *Allosaurus*, the orbital crests (the crests above its eyes) were smaller and more pointed. A raised ridge running down the center of the snout was also present, and the jaws were filled with approximately sixty thin, serrated, and blade-like teeth.

Zuniceratops
(zoo-knee-s-air-uh-tops)

Name Meaning: Zuni-Horned Face
Order: Ornithischia
Kind: Ceratopsidae
Habitat: Western North America
Diet: Herbivore
Height: 3.5-4 feet
Length: 10-11.5 feet

One of the smallest of the ceratopsians, *Zuniceratops* lived in what is now the south-western United States. *Zuniceratops* was proportioned in the same way as other, larger ceratopsians, but on a smaller scale. Its large frill was around the same length as the rest of its skull, and had two large holes, one on each side, called **fenestra** (fen-est-ruh).

Adorning the front of the animal's skull was a pair of large brow horns, as seen in many other species of ceratopsians. The horns of *Zuniceratops* curved gradually upward. Like all ceratopsians, these large horns were covered by a layer of keratin. This is the same material that makes up our hair and fingernails. This covering of keratin would have made the horns longer and sharper.

Paleontologists believe that *Zuniceratops* and other ceratopsians would have used their horns not only as a way to recognize individuals, but also for fighting and defense. Horns of many ceratopsian specimens have been found with broken tips, scrapes, and other evidence of trauma. A famous *Triceratops* specimen found in Montana in 2014 named "Big John," has a large hole on the right side of its frill that appears to have come from the horn of another *Triceratops*. Remarkably, the injury appeared to be in the process of healing at the time of Big John's death.

It's likely that many ceratopsians fought amongst each other for dominance and mating rights, similar to the sparring seen amongst deer today. It is also believed that these animals would have used their horns in order to defend themselves from large predators, or groups of smaller predators.

Unlike many members of its kind, *Zuniceratops* lacked any sort of nasal horn. Instead, it had a long and flat snout. Like all ceratopsians, the front of its skull ended in a large beak, similar to the beaks seen in turtles. The upper beak bone, called the **rostral**, would help to clip leaves and other types of vegetation off of plants. Inside its mouth, there were dozens of leaf-shaped teeth for cutting up plant material for the animal to swallow.

Dinosaur Archives

Dinosaurs Aboard the Ark:

Would dinosaurs really have been on Noah's ark? The answer to this question is a resounding absolutely! Scripture is very clear when it tells us in Genesis 6: 19-20,

And of every living thing of all flesh, you shall bring two of every sort into the ark to keep them alive with you. They shall be male and female. Of the birds, according to their **kinds**, and of the animals, according their **kinds**, of every creeping thing of the ground, according to its **kind**, two of every sort shall come in to you to keep them alive.

The Bible tells us that a pair (seven of some) of every kind of land-dwelling, air-breathing animal were brought onto the ark, along with Noah and his family. There is no logical reason to assume that dinosaurs would have been excluded from this. We know dinosaurs were still around by the time of the flood because we still find their fossils today. If they had died out long before the flood, any evidence of their existence would have been wiped out by the violent and catastrophic conditions of the worldwide flood.

But, could they even fit? Again, absolutely! The max number of dinosaur kinds is likely between fifty to eighty. Therefore, even in a worst-case scenario, Noah only needed about 160 dinosaurs on the ark. The ark, measuring 510 feet long, eighty-five feet wide, and about fifty-one feet tall, had plenty of room for two of EVERY kind of animal needed on the ark, including the dinosaurs.

Size was also not an issue because many dinosaurs were already small. Also, it is possible that God sent juveniles (young adults) of these animals to Noah.

This would be beneficial for many reasons, such as:

1. Younger animals take up less space.

2. Younger animals require smaller quantities of food and water.

3. Younger animals will produce less waste.

4. Younger animals have a longer life ahead of them, and therefore are better suited to repopulate the earth after the flood.

Because of these reasons and more, it is very likely that God indeed sent juveniles of all the animals on the ark, and not only the dinosaurs.

After their time aboard the ark (which lasted about one year), Noah and his family, as well as all of the animals aboard the ark, came off of the ark and entered a new and mysterious world, a world very different from the one they left behind.

Dinosaurs After The Global Flood:

Along with all of the other animals that departed from the ark, two of every kind of dinosaur did as well. The post-flood world they entered into was vastly different from the pre-flood world they had known. They would face many new trials in this "New World."

Slowly, and as time went on, these magnificent creatures seem to have faded away, until there were none left on the face of the earth. Potential reasons for their demise are plentiful, a few being competition with other animals, including competition for food and territory. Loss of food sources likely played a part, with some plants that the herbivorous dinosaurs ate potentially having gone extinct during the great flood. Another factor that likely played a huge role in driving these animals to extinction was hunting. Mankind potentially hunted the herbivorous dinosaurs for food, or even for sport. The carnivorous dinosaurs were likely hunted for sport as well, or for the protection of livestock, and possibly simply out of fear.

These reasons, among others, seem to have driven these animals to extinction. However, we are not God, and therefore, we cannot search everywhere at the same time. So, could there still be a living dinosaur in some unexplored region of the globe? Possibly. Though as far as we know, all representatives of this unique group of reptiles have sadly gone extinct.

However, countless evidence indicates that dinosaurs lived for a significant amount of time after the flood. But if they did, then why don't we see the word "dinosaur" in history books or ancient writings? The answer to this question is actually quite simple. The word "dinosaur" was not invented until 1841, when it was coined by a Christian anatomist named

Sir Richard Owen. This word originally meaning "fearfully great lizard," has since been re-interpreted to mean "terrible lizard." It is worth noting that dinosaurs are indeed not lizards, they are a unique group of reptiles. However, the word lizard has historically been used to describe many different types of reptiles, other than true lizards.

Before the word "dinosaur" existed, the word "dragon" was used to describe many different types of reptiles, including the bones of dinosaurs. Though beyond the range of this book, it is important to know that many legends, historical accounts, paintings, and carvings from around the world describe and depict dragons of many different sorts: flying dragons, swimming dragons, and land-dwelling dragons. Many of these land-dwelling dragons resemble animals that today we would call dinosaurs. In fact, the *Epic of Beowulf*, and the legend of *St. George and the Dragon*, both seem to describe a spinosaurid like dinosaur, possibly inspired by a *Suchomimus* or a *Baryonyx*. A large number of dragon accounts end with the dragon being killed, adding further weight to the theory that many dinosaurs were indeed hunted by man.

Dragons, including at least one dinosaur, are mentioned numerous times throughout the Bible as well. There are multiple mentions of flying dragons (pterosaurs), sea dragons (marine reptiles), and land dragons (dinosaurs and other land reptiles). The Behemoth mentioned in Job 40:15-24 is described as "first of the works of God," and making "his tail stiff like a cedar." The rest of the passage describes many other mighty features of this animal. An honest examination of the animal kingdom, both living and extinct, demonstrates that nothing fits this description better than a sauropod dinosaur.

When we take an honest look at the world around us regarding dinosaurs, and any other subject, we see that both science and history really do confirm the Bible!

Glossary

- *Apatosaurus:* a large sauropod dinosaur, often mis-labeled Brontosaurus.

- *Baryonyx:* a mid-sized member of the spinosaur kind discovered in Europe.

- **Collagen fibers:** a type of protein commonly found in connective tissues like muscle and skin.

- **Denticles:** small bumps or serrations on some teeth that give the tooth a serrated edge.

- *Dimorphodon:* a small pterosaur with a large skull, found in England.

- **Dorsal:** Opposite of ventral, used to refer to the back of an animal, i.e. the dorsal fin of a shark.

- *Dsungaripterus:* a pterosaur from eastern Asia with an upturned beak, and a large crest running down its snout.

- **Epoccipitals:** large horn-like protrusions made of bone, found lining the frills of many ceratopsians.

- **Facultative biped:** an animal that primarily walks on all fours, but one that is capable of walking exclusively on its hind legs if necessary.

- **Fenestra:** a natural hole in the bone of an animal.

- *Gallimimus:* a mid-sized theropod with a long neck, and long legs designed for fast running.

- *Gastroliths*: stones that are swallowed by some animals in order to help grind up food.

- *Hesperornis:* a small, extinct, flightless bird found in the western United States.

- **Ichthyosaur:** marine reptiles characterized by their dolphin-like appearance, and classified in the order ichthyosauria.

- *Ichthyosaurus:* one of the smallest ichthyosaurs, and the one after which the order gets its name.

- **Infraorder:** a level of taxonomic classification that ranks below a suborder, and above a superfamily.

- **Kind:** a biblical unit of classification, which most often correlates to the family level of modern taxonomy.

- **Mammoth:** a large, extinct mammal, covered in long fur, belonging to the elephant kind.

- **Marginocephalia:** one of three suborders of the order ornithischia. This suborder contains the ceratopsians and the pachycephalosaurs.

- **Ornithischia:** the order of dinosaurs with rear-facing pubic (singular: pubis) bones, rear-facing ischia (singular: ischium), and ilea (singular: ileum) that lie horizontally, like a roof. Note: exceptions to the rear-pointing pubic bones do exist.

- **Ornithopoda:** one of three suborders of the order ornithischia. This suborder includes the iguanodontids, the hadrosaurs, and a few other groups of ornithischian dinosaurs.

- **Ossicle:** a small osteoderm less than one centimeter in diameter.

- **Osteoderm:** a bone growing in the skin of an animal, and not directly attached to the rest of the animal's skeleton.

- **Pigment:** natural substances which produce color in the tissues of living things.

- **Piscivore:** a specialized type of carnivore that primarily hunts and eats fish.

- **Plesiosaur:** marine reptiles characterized by paddle-like flippers and long sauropod-like necks.

- **Pterosaur:** flying reptiles, often incorrectly called pterodactyls.

- *Quetzalcoatlus:* a large pterosaur, which was the largest flying animal known to exist.

- *Repenomamus robustus:* a small extinct mammal found in China that shares some similarities with today's Tasmanian devil. This animal has been found with the remains of a young *Psittacosaurus* contained in its stomach.

- **Reptilia:** the class of vertebrate animals consisting of all living and extinct reptiles.

- *Rhamphorhynchus:* a small pterosaur with an upturned snout, filled with dozens of needle-like teeth.

- **Rostral:** a term used to describe the upper beak bone found in ceratopsian dinosaurs.

- *Sanajeh:* a large, extinct snake found in India that is thought to have preyed upon dinosaur hatchlings.

- *Sarcosuchus:* a large, extinct, and thin-snouted crocodile from northern Africa.

- **Saurischia:** the order of dinosaurs with forward-facing pubic (singular: pubis) bones, rear-facing ischia (singular: ischium), and ilea (singular: ileum), that stand vertically like a wall. Note: exceptions to the forward-pointing pubic bones do exist.

- **Sauropodomorpha**: one of two suborders of the order saurischia. This suborder contains all sauropodomorphs, i.e., the sauropods and prosauropods.

- *Stegosaurus:* the largest species of stegosaur, and the one for which the family is named.

- **Suborder:** a level of taxonomic classification that ranks below an order, and above an infraorder.

- **Taxonomy:** a scientific classification system developed by Carl Linnaeus, and used to classify living things into a kingdom, phylum, class, order, family, genus, and species.

- **Thagomizer:** the four large tails spikes made of bone, found on the tails of stegosaurs.

- **Theropoda:** one of two suborders of the order saurischia. This suborder contains all dinosaurs known as theropods.

- **Thyreophora:** one of three suborders of the order ornithischia. This suborder contains the ankylosaurs and stegosaurs.

- *Triceratops:* the largest and most well-known member of the group of dinosaurs known as ceratopsians.

- **Vertebrate:** an animal with a backbone.

CPSIA information can be obtained
at www.ICGtesting.com
Printed in the USA
BVHW091451091122
651395BV00001BB/14